A LEARNING WORKS SKILL BUILDER

HANDWRITING HAMBURGER

WRITTEN BY LINDA SCHWARTZ **ILLUSTRATED BY BEV ARMSTRONG**

© THE LEARNING WORKS

The Learning Works

Copyright © 1979 - The Learning Works
All rights reserved.
Printed in the United States of America.

HANDWRITING HAMBURGER

FEATURES OF HANDWRITING HAMBURGER

1. *Handwriting Hamburger* provides instruction, practice, and review in making all twenty-six cursive letters, both upper- and lower-case.

2. A chart shows the proper formation of the entire alphabet. The book also provides tips on good·handwriting, a Super Six Checklist of specific things to look for in your handwriting, and an individual progress chart to score as each lesson is completed.

HOW TO USE HANDWRITING HAMBURGER

1. The correct letter formation is shown for both the upper- and lower-case letter in the top corner of each page. Study the letters carefully.

2. Space is provided for you to practice writing each letter. Begin by tracing the letter with your pencil for practice. Then fill in the dotted letter for additional practice. Now write the letter on your own. Write your best cursive upper- and lower-case letters in the boxes titled, "My Best."

3. A tongue-twister sentence is given for each letter of the alphabet. Notice how the letters are shaped.

4. Lines are provided at the bottom of each page. Copy the tongue-twister in your neatest cursive writing.

5. When you finish each page, check your writing with the checklist on page 4.

6. Record your progress according to the directions on page 5.

✱ THE ALPHABET ✱

Aa Bb Cc Dd Ee

Ff Gg Hh Ii Jj

Kk Ll Mm Nn Oo

Pp Qq Rr Ss Tt

Uu Vv Ww Xx Yy

Zz

✶ SUPER SIX CHECKLIST ✶

THIS   **NOT THIS**

1. SIZE
  Are all similar letters the same height? (Use your ruler to find out.)

2. SHAPE
  Are the shapes of your letters the same as the models on page 3?

3. SLANT
  Are all your letters slanted to the right and parallel to each other?

4. SPACING
  Did you leave space between the <u>letters</u>?
  Did you leave uniform spacing between <u>words</u>?

5. RESTING ON THE BASE LINE
  Are all your letters touching the base line?

6. NEATNESS
  Is your writing neat and clean?

✶ HANDWRITING HAMBURGER HINTS ✶

1. In cursive writing, each letter is made without taking your pencil or pen from the paper.

2. The small i's and j's are dotted, and the t's and x's are crossed <u>after</u> your word is written. *taxi taxi*

3. Each letter should be completed with the proper end stroke shown on page 3.

© THE LEARNING WORKS

HANDWRITING HAMBURGER
✳ PROGRESS CHART ✳

This is a chart to record your progress as you work in the <u>Handwriting Hamburger</u>. After each lesson, ask yourself the checklist questions found on page 4. Place a ✓ in each square where you feel your handwriting is satisfactory. Go back and practice the letters that give you problems.

PAGE	7	8	9	10	11	12	13	14	15	16	17	18	19
SIZE													
SHAPE													
SLANT													
SPACING													
RESTING ON BASE LINE													
NEATNESS													

PAGE	20	21	22	23	24	25	26	27	28	29	30	31	32
SIZE													
SHAPE													
SLANT													
SPACING													
RESTING ON BASE LINE													
NEATNESS													

© THE LEARNING WORKS

✷✷✷✷ HANDWRITING HANG-UPS ✷✷✷✷

These are some of the letters that cause the most problems in cursive writing. Practice writing each letter.

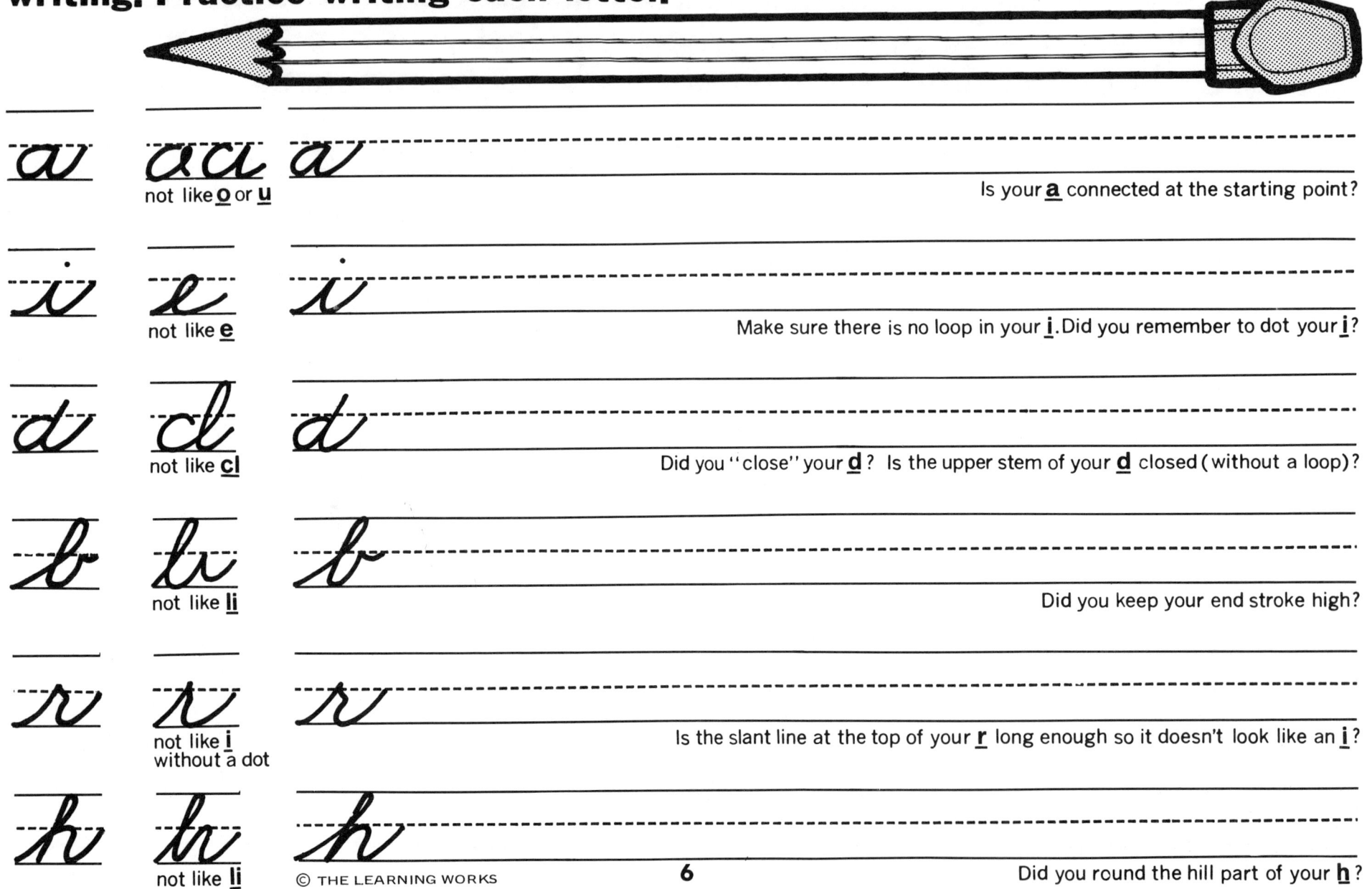

a   *aa*   *a*
not like **o** or **u**

Is your **a** connected at the starting point?

i   *e*   *i*
not like **e**

Make sure there is no loop in your **i**. Did you remember to dot your **i**?

d   *cl*   *d*
not like **cl**

Did you "close" your **d**? Is the upper stem of your **d** closed (without a loop)?

b   *li*   *b*
not like **li**

Did you keep your end stroke high?

r   *r*   *r*
not like **i** without a dot

Is the slant line at the top of your **r** long enough so it doesn't look like an **i**?

h   *li*   *h*
not like **li**

Did you round the hill part of your **h**?

© THE LEARNING WORKS

Aa Aa

Name _____

MY BEST ☐ *Aa* MY BEST ☐

Amy Aardvark attacked an amazing amount of ants.

Now it's your turn! Copy the sentence above in your best writing.

© THE LEARNING WORKS

B b B b

Name _____

MY BEST ☐   MY BEST ☐

B b   b b

The black bat blew bunches of big bubbles in Bolivia.

Now it's your turn! Copy the sentence above in your best writing.

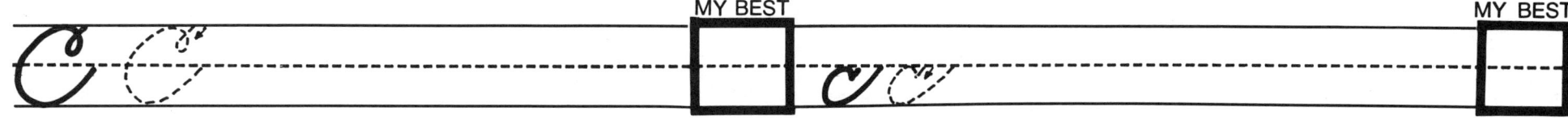

Name_____

Contented camels calmly chew cotton candy in Cairo.

Dd Dd

Name _____

D d

Dragons do disco dancing in downtown Denver daily.

E e E e

Name

Ed, the electric eel, escaped with eighteen extra eclairs.

Name _____

Ff Ff

Ff ff

The Friday fish fry features famous fried flounder.

G g   G g

Name _____

MY BEST ☐

G g   g g

MY BEST ☐

A greedy goose gagged after grabbing George's gingerbread.

Hh Hh

H H   MY BEST   *h h*   MY BEST

Name _____

Hank Hippo happily inhaled a hundred huge hamburgers.

Ii Ii

I I ii

Igor, the immense iguana, invented India ink.

Name _____

J j   J j

MY BEST ☐   *J j*   **MY BEST** ☐

Joyous Jill Jackrabbit juggles jingle bells in January.

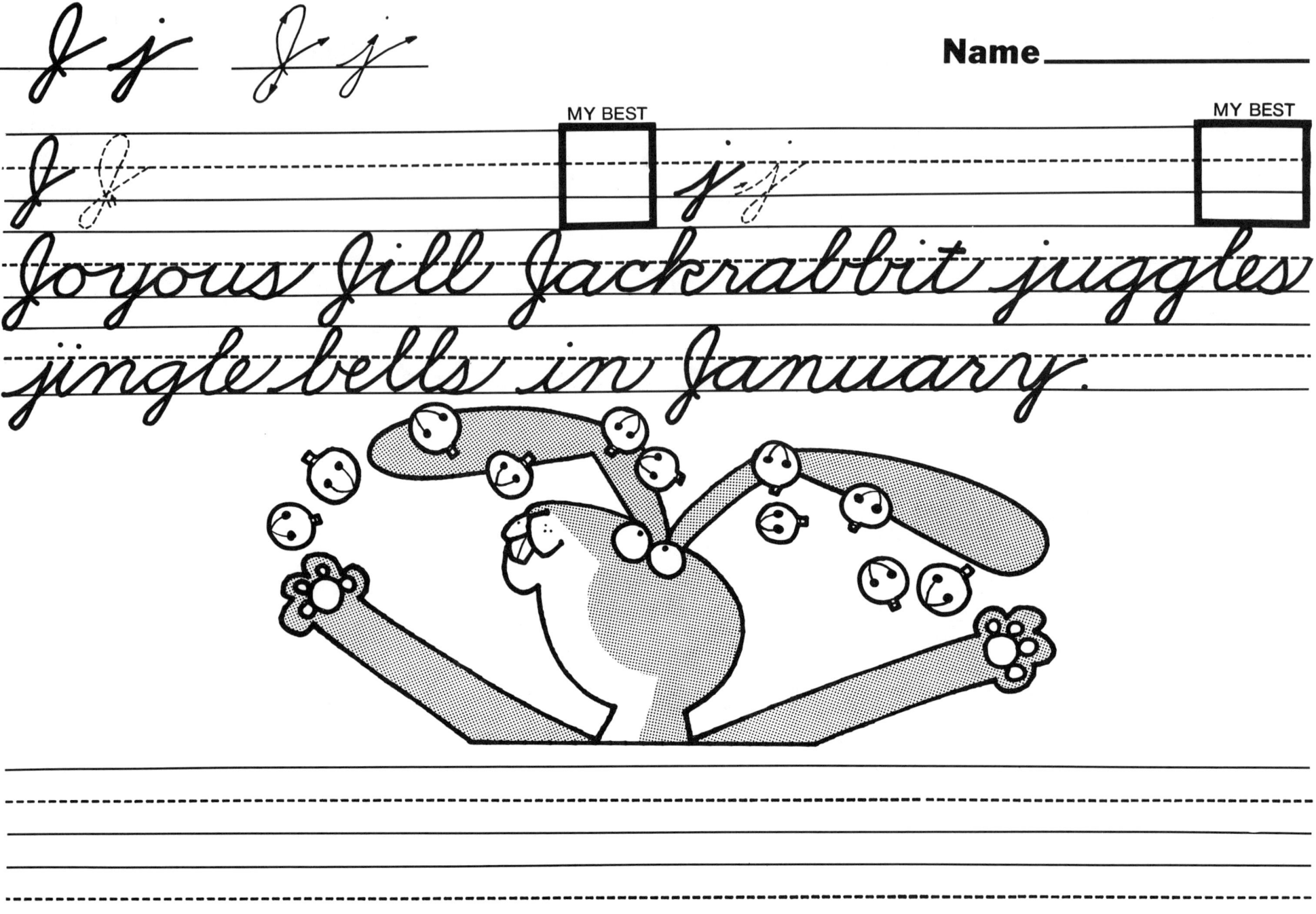

Kk Kk

Name _____

Kk   MY BEST ☐   *k k*   MY BEST ☐

Katie Kiwi kept her kazoo in a pink wicker basket.

L l L l

L L l l

Leon, the lovable llama, licked lollipops in Lima.

Mm Mm

Name_____

MY BEST ☐   MY BEST ☐

M M   m m

Many mad moose marched in Miami at midnight.

Nn Nn

Nn   *nn*

Name _____

MY BEST ☐   MY BEST ☐

The nearsighted nanny did not notice the Newfoundland

20

Oo Oo

Name_____

Oo o

Oscar, the obese old octopus,
outweighed an octet of owls.

P p *P p*

P p

Pete Piranha put pepper on a perfect pumpkin pie.

Q q Q q

Name _____

MY BEST ☐   MY BEST ☐

Q Q   q q

The quail quartet from quaint Quito quit quarreling.

Name _____

Rr Rr

Rr

A rare royal rhinoceros ran through the rain in Rome.

Ss Ss

Name _____

S   □ MY BEST   *s*   □ MY BEST

Six silly sheep skated slowly south to San Francisco.

Tt Tt

Name _____

Tt   MY BEST   *tt*   MY BEST

Three tired toads toted tin tubas to Tahiti today.

Uu Uu

Uu   u u

Ulysses Unicorn plunked his ukulele underwater in Utah.

Name_____

Vivian Vulture viciously viewed a very vain viper.

Ww Ww

Ww ww

Name _____

MY BEST ☐   MY BEST ☐

Wendy Walrus wore a weird wig every Wednesday.

Name _____

X x X x

MY BEST ☐   *X X*   *x x*   MY BEST ☐

Xavier Fox examined sixteen boxes of xylophones.

Y y *Y* *y*

Name _____

MY BEST ☐   MY BEST ☐

Y y *y y*

Yesterday a yak yanked a yellow yo-yo in Yonkers.

Name_____

MY BEST

MY BEST

Zelda, the zany zebra, went zipping through the zoo.